J 636.1
Hudak
Hudak, Heather C.

Ponies

Farm Animals
Ponies

Heather C. Hudak

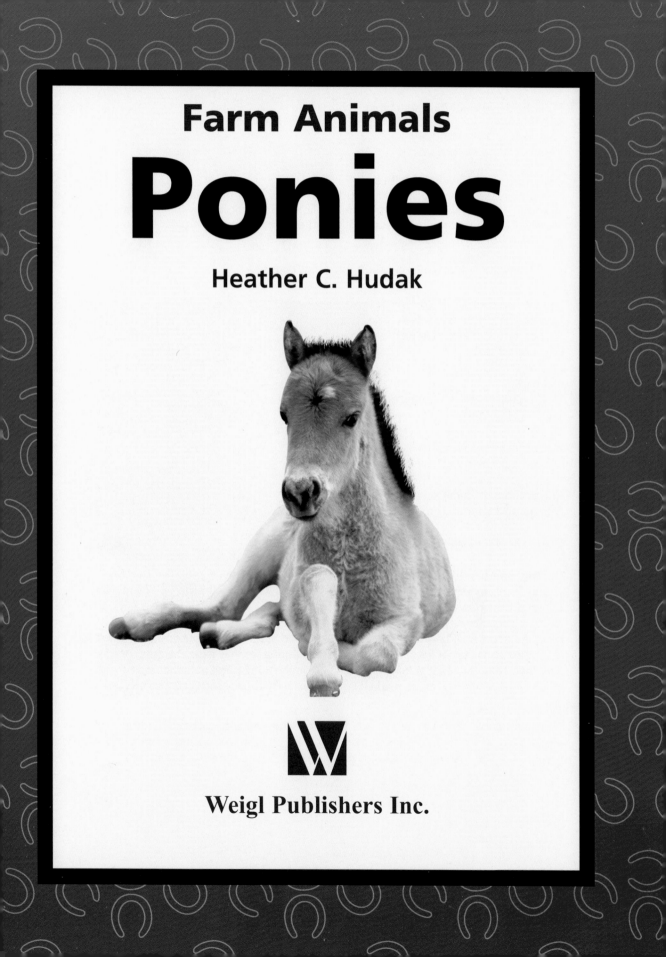

Weigl Publishers Inc.

Published by Weigl Publishers Inc.
350 5th Avenue, Suite 3304, PMB 6G
New York, NY 10118-0069
Website: www.weigl.com

Library of Congress Cataloging-in-Publication Data

Hudak, Heather C., 1975-
  Ponies / Heather C. Hudak.
      p. cm. -- (Farm animals)
  Includes index.
  ISBN 1-59036-426-0 (hard cover : alk. paper) -- ISBN 1-59036-433-3 (soft cover :
alk. paper)
  1. Ponies--Juvenile literature. I. Title.
  SF315.H83 2007
                                    2005034671
Printed in the United States of America
1 2 3 4 5 6 7 8 9 0 10 09 08 07 06

Editor Frances Purslow
Design and Layout Terry Paulhus

Cover: Shetland ponies were first bred in Scotland.

Photograph Credits: North Wind Picture Archives / Alamy: page 20; Courtesy
Judith Durr an artist inspired by her Choctaw and Cherokee heritage. "Mud Pony"
is based on an American Indian myth: page 21.

All of the Internet URLs given in the book were valid at the time of publication. However,
due to the dynamic nature of the Internet, some addresses may have changed, or sites
may have ceased to exist since publication. While the author and publisher regret any
inconvenience this may cause readers, no responsibility for any such changes can be
accepted by either the author or the publisher.

Every reasonable effort has been made to trace ownership and to obtain permission to
reprint copyright material. The publishers would be pleased to have any errors or omissions
brought to their attention so that they may be corrected in subsequent printings.

Contents

Meet the Pony

Ponies are small horses. They stand less than 57 inches (1.5 meters) tall. Ponies have pointy ears and long **muzzles**. They have hairy coats, long **manes**, and long tails.

Ponies are mammals. Mother ponies feed their young with milk from their bodies. Like most mammals, ponies have hair on their bodies.

Ponies are social animals. Many live in large groups called herds. In herds, some ponies are leaders, while others are followers. The leaders are the first to access food, water, and mates.

To measure ponies, people use units called hands. Each "hand" is equal to 4 inches (0.10 m). Ponies are measured from the ground to the top of their **withers**.

Assateague Island, off the coast of Maryland, is well known for the wild ponies that live there. They are called Chincoteague ponies.

All about Ponies

Ponies are smart. They learn quickly, so they are easy to train. They can be taught to wear a saddle or pull a cart. They can even learn to respond to short words.

Ponies are **sensitive** animals. They are easily frightened. Sudden noises or unexpected movements can startle them.

Ponies come in different colors, shapes, and sizes. There are many **breeds** of ponies. Different pony breeds can be found all over the world.

The way a pony walks or runs is called its gait.

Breeds of Ponies

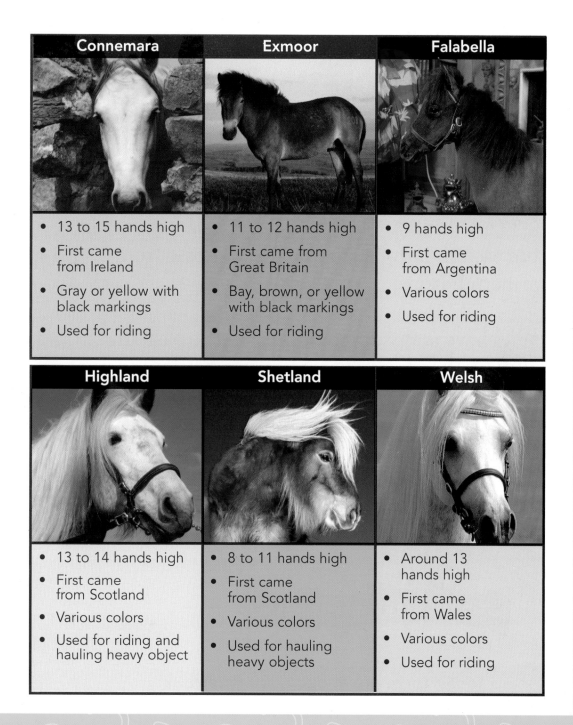

Connemara

- 13 to 15 hands high
- First came from Ireland
- Gray or yellow with black markings
- Used for riding

Exmoor

- 11 to 12 hands high
- First came from Great Britain
- Bay, brown, or yellow with black markings
- Used for riding

Falabella

- 9 hands high
- First came from Argentina
- Various colors
- Used for riding

Highland

- 13 to 14 hands high
- First came from Scotland
- Various colors
- Used for riding and hauling heavy object

Shetland

- 8 to 11 hands high
- First came from Scotland
- Various colors
- Used for hauling heavy objects

Welsh

- Around 13 hands high
- First came from Wales
- Various colors
- Used for riding

Pony History

Horses belong to the *Equidae family*. Equidae have existed for more than 50 million years. All tame horses and ponies today come from three breeds of horses that lived between 10,000 and 2.5 million years ago. Those are the Przewalski's horse from central Asia, the tarpan from eastern Europe, and the forest horse from northern Europe.

Ponies have many different uses. In the past, they pulled carts and carried armies into battle. Today, some people use ponies as pack animals to carry goods. Others ride ponies for fun and for sport. Some people even keep ponies as guides.

Today, there are about 1,000 Przewalski horses in the world.

In the Himalayan mountains, ponies are often used as pack animals to help travelers.

Pony Shelter

Many ponies live on farms. Most farm ponies live outdoors. They **graze** on large, open fields of grass called pastures.

Outdoor ponies need shelters that provide protection from poor weather. Pony shelters should be dry and clean. They should also have doors that allow ponies to come and go as they please.

Some ponies, such as show and riding ponies, are indoor animals. They stay in barns with stalls. Staying indoors keeps ponies clean and safe from injury. Each stall should have clean sawdust or straw bedding for ponies.

Ponies are good companions for children. Caring for ponies teaches children to be responsible.

Shetland ponies are strong, but gentle, animals.

Pony Features

Ponies communicate with each other by making different sounds. They snort to warn other ponies of dangers. They nicker when they are around other horses or humans they know. They neigh when they are trying to find other horses or tell others they are nearby.

A pony's body is **adapted** to living on open plains and pasture. In autumn, ponies grow heavy winter coats to keep warm. They shed these coats in the spring. Ponies also have strong, muscular legs to help them travel long distances.

FEET
Ponies have hoofed feet. Hooves are horn-like shells that protect the soft parts of a pony's feet.

MANE AND FORELOCK
Ponies have long, wiry hair that grows along the back of their neck and up toward the front of their head.

EYES
Ponies and horses have the largest eyes of any land mammal. Their eyes are located on the sides of their head. They can see almost all the way away around themselves.

NOSE
Ponies have a better sense of smell than humans. They can tell one person or animal from another by its smell.

EARS
Ponies express their feelings by moving their ears. When their ears point up and face forward, the pony is happy and interested. Flicking ears show that the pony is listening.

What Do Ponies Eat?

Ponies are herbivores. Herbivores eat plants. Ponies eat grass, hay, and grains. Carrots and sugar cubes are treats for ponies. They also need fresh water nearby.

Working ponies need high-energy feed, such as special grains and hay. These ponies need soft, green hay to eat. It should have a sweet smell and be clean. Moldy hay can be harmful to ponies.

In winter, ponies need to gain weight to keep warm. Eating certain foods, such as rice bran, can help ponies gain weight.

Fascinating Facts

Younger ponies should be kept in their own feeding stall. Sometimes they chase away older ponies or eat more quickly. This keeps older ponies from eating enough food.

Chincoteague ponies eat salt marsh grass and beach grass. The high amount of salt in their diet causes them to drink twice as much water as tame ponies.

Pony Life Cycle

Mother ponies are called mares. Father ponies are called stallions. Baby ponies are called foals.

Mares carry their babies in their bellies for about 11 months. Most mares have one baby at a time. The process of giving birth is called foaling.

Newborn

At birth, a foal's legs are almost full-grown. Foals can begin to walk about 20 minutes after they are born.

Mares feed their foals milk from their body. It has many nutrients to help the foal grow big and strong.

6 Months to 2 Years Old

When ponies are 4 to 6 months old, they stop drinking milk from their mother. This is called weaning. Weaning takes about 6 weeks.

Once weaned, foals begin to eat grain, hay, and grass.

Most foals are born in the spring. They grow quickly. Male foals are called colts, and female foals are called fillies.

Ponies and horses live for 24 to 30 years. Ponies often live longer than large horses.

Adult

Ponies are full-grown at 3 years of age. At the withers, they grow between 49 and 57 inches (1.2 and 1.5 m) tall. Adult ponies weigh between 400 and 700 pounds (181 and 317 kg).

Caring for Ponies

Ponies need special care. They must visit the veterinarian, or animal doctor, at least once a year. Ponies need to be given **vaccinations**, too. Every two months, ponies need special medicine to keep away **parasites**. Proper dental care is also important.

Ponies must be groomed each day. They should be brushed along their backs and under their bellies. This keeps their skin clean of dirt.

Stones can bruise ponies' feet. They must be removed from the hooves. If stones are not removed, they can cause a disease called thrush. A farrier, or horseshoe maker, should clip ponies' hooves every two or three months.

Useful Websites

To find out more about caring for ponies visit: **www.mda.state.mi.us/kids**. Click on "Country Fair," then "Animals," and "Ponies."

To clean a pony's hooves, run your hand down the bottom half of the back of its leg so it will lift its foot.

Myths and Legends

For centuries, people around the world have shared many tales about ponies. There is a Russian **fable** called *The Humpbacked Pony*. It teaches people that bad things happen to those who are selfish and greedy. In Irish legends, ponies are a symbol of power and speed.

Ponies appear as magical creatures in American Indian legends.

The Mud Pony

A retelling of a traditional American Indian tale describes a magical pony that was created from clay.

There was a poor boy who loved ponies. He would make ponies out of mud. One night he dreamed about a pony. In the dream, the pony said, "My son, you are poor, and Mother Earth has given me to you." When the boy awoke, he saw one of his mud ponies pawing the ground and tossing its mane. The pony had come to life. The Mud Pony did not need to eat or drink. All the boy had to do was cover the pony with a blanket each night to protect it from the rain.

While riding his pony, the boy hunted more buffalo than the other men. In war, no one could hurt him, and he always won. Years later, the boy became chief. One night, the chief forgot to cover his pony with a blanket. He had a dream that his pony said, "My son, you are no longer poor. I am returning to Mother Earth."

When the chief awoke, it was raining hard. He ran to his pony, but it was too late. On the hillside, he saw a pile of mud, still in the shape of a pony.

Frequently Asked Questions

What is colic?

Answer: Colic is a strong stomach pain in horses and ponies. It is caused by sudden changes in their diet. Colic is the most common pony stomach problem. Ponies should see a veterinarian if the pain lasts more than a day.

How do I bathe my pony?

Answer: First, groom the pony to remove tangles from its tail and mane. Then, bathe the pony with warm water and human or animal shampoo. Use a cotton cloth called a stable rubber to dry the pony. Bathing should be done every few days.

How do I know if my pony is bored?

Answer: Boredom can cause a pony to form bad habits. Some ponies use their teeth to grab onto stalls or feeders. This is called crib-biting. Proper exercise and grooming can make a pony happy and less bored.

Puzzler

See if you can answer these questions about ponies.

1. What are three pony breeds?
2. Where did the first tamed horse come from?
3. What can ponies be used for?
4. What do ponies eat?
5. Where do ponies live?

Answers: 1. Connemara, Exmoor, Shetland, Welsh, Highland, Falabella 2. Central Asia 3. For riding and hauling heavy things 4. Grass, hay, grains, carrots, sugar cubes, and rice bran 5. On farms and on pastures

Find Out More

There are many more interesting facts to learn about ponies. If you would like to learn more, take a look at these books.

Draper, Judith and Elwyn Hartley Edwards. *My First Horse and Pony Care Book*. London, UK: Kingfisher, 2006.

Walter Gilbrey. *Ponies Past and Present*. Alcester, UK: Read Country Books, 2005.

Words to Know

adapted: adjusted to the natural environment

breeds: groups of animals that have common features

fable: a short story that teaches a lesson

family: any group of living things that share common features

graze: to eat grass in a field

manes: long hair on ponies' necks and backs

muzzles: the nose and jaw area of animals

parasites: living things that feed off and live on other living things

sensitive: reacts quickly to sudden motion, noise, and fear

vaccinations: medicines that prevent illness

withers: the base of a pony's neck

Index